U.S.A. TRAVEL GUIDES

KENTUCKY

BY ANN HEINRICHS • ILLUSTRATED BY MATT KANIA

The Child's World®
childsworld.com

Published by The Child's World®
1980 Lookout Drive • Mankato, MN 56003-1705
800-599-READ • www.childsworld.com

ISBN 9781503819573
LCCN 2016961133

Printing
Printed in the United States of America
PA02334

Ann Heinrichs is the author of more than 100 books for children and young adults. She has also enjoyed successful careers as a children's book editor and an advertising copywriter. Ann grew up in Fort Smith, Arkansas, and lives in Chicago, Illinois.

About the Author
Ann Heinrichs

Matt Kania loves maps and, as a kid, dreamed of making them. In school he studied geography and cartography, and today he makes maps for a living. Matt's favorite thing about drawing maps is learning about the places they represent. Many of the maps he has created can be found in books, magazines, videos, Web sites, and public places.

About the
Map Illustrator
Matt Kania

On the cover: Kentucky horses relax in a field.

OUR KENTUCKY TRIP

Ready for a tour of the Bluegrass State? That's Kentucky! Just follow the car on that dotted line. Or else skip around. Either way, you'll have lots of fun. You'll learn some amazing things, too.

You'll explore caves and coal mines. You'll cheer your favorite racehorse. You'll enjoy a taste of **pioneer** life. And you'll even get to know Daniel Boone.

Are you ready? Then buckle up, and let's hit the road!

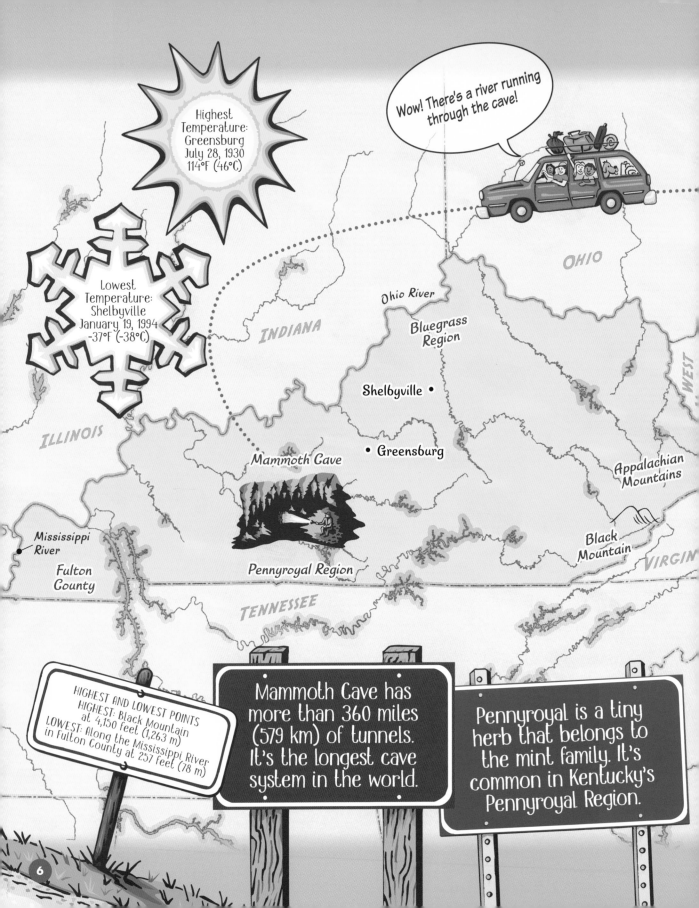

TOURING MAMMOTH CAVE

Tighten up your **hard hat**. Strap on those knee pads, too. You're taking the Wild Cave Tour in Mammoth Cave!

Mammoth Cave is Kentucky's most famous natural site. It's in the Pennyroyal Region in south-central Kentucky. The Bluegrass Region is in north-central Kentucky. Lots of horses and cattle graze there.

Many mountains rise in eastern Kentucky. They're part of the Appalachian mountain range.

Big rivers create some of Kentucky's borders. The Ohio River outlines its entire northern border. The Mississippi River forms the western border.

Ready for a workout? Tour Mammoth Cave! It's the longest cave in the world.

THE DANIEL BOONE FESTIVAL IN BARBOURVILLE

Put on your **breeches** and hunting shirt. It's the Daniel Boone Festival in Barbourville!

This festival celebrates **frontiersman** Daniel Boone. He explored the Cumberland Gap Region. He wanted to cut a wide trail there. Then pioneers could move west of the Appalachians.

Boone helped build the Wilderness Road in 1775. He knew the road cut through Cherokee land. He met with the Cherokees. They agreed Boone could buy land from them. Soon thousands of pioneers poured into Kentucky. Boone guided many of them.

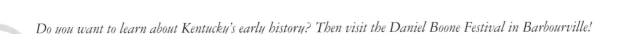

Do you want to learn about Kentucky's early history? Then visit the Daniel Boone Festival in Barbourville!

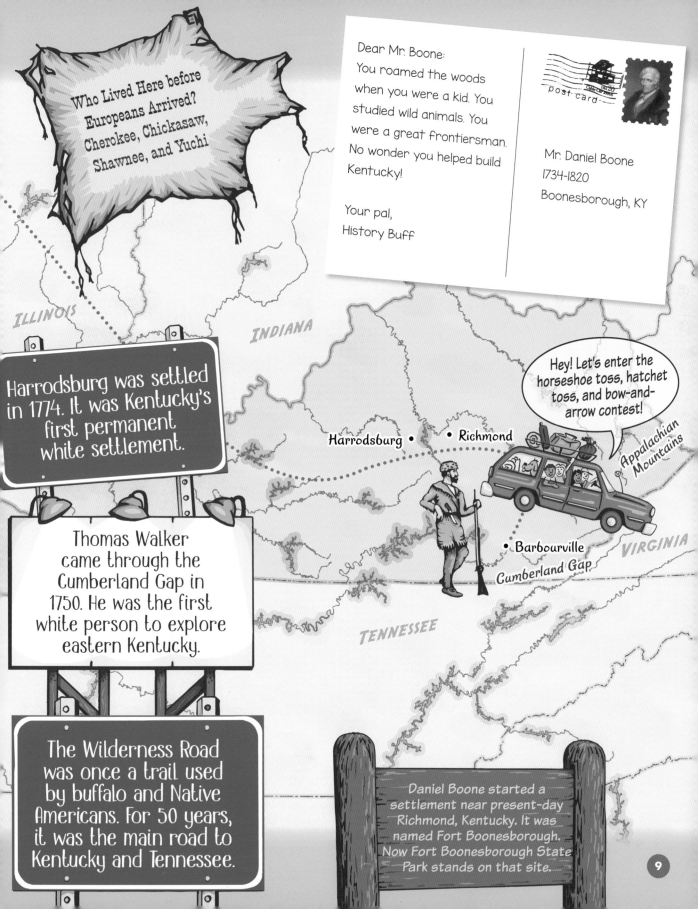

Who Lived Here before Europeans Arrived? Cherokee, Chickasaw, Shawnee, and Yuchi

Dear Mr. Boone:
You roamed the woods when you were a kid. You studied wild animals. You were a great frontiersman. No wonder you helped build Kentucky!

Your pal,
History Buff

post card

Mr. Daniel Boone
1734-1820
Boonesborough, KY

Harrodsburg was settled in 1774. It was Kentucky's first permanent white settlement.

Thomas Walker came through the Cumberland Gap in 1750. He was the first white person to explore eastern Kentucky.

The Wilderness Road was once a trail used by buffalo and Native Americans. For 50 years, it was the main road to Kentucky and Tennessee.

Hey! Let's enter the horseshoe toss, hatchet toss, and bow-and-arrow contest!

ILLINOIS
INDIANA
Harrodsburg • • Richmond
Appalachian Mountains
• Barbourville VIRGINIA
Cumberland Gap
TENNESSEE

Daniel Boone started a settlement near present-day Richmond, Kentucky. It was named Fort Boonesborough. Now Fort Boonesborough State Park stands on that site.

STATE FLOWER
GOLDENROD

STATE TREE
TULIP POPLAR

STATE BIRD
CARDINAL

Guess what? Land Between the Lakes is between two lakes. Duh! The lakes are Kentucky Lake and Lake Barkley.

OHIO

ILLINOIS

INDIANA

WEST

Henderson

Land Between the Lakes

Kentucky Lake

Lake Barkley

The Barrens

VIRGINIA

TENNESSEE

Vast grasslands once covered south-central Kentucky. Few trees grew there. Early explorers called this region the Barrens.

John James Audubon was a bird expert. The John James Audubon Park Museum & Nature Center in Henderson features his artwork and writings.

The National Park Service has five sites in Kentucky.

Land Between the Lakes has a herd of fallow deer. These small deer are originally from Europe and Asia. They run with a stiff-legged bounce.

Huge bison, or buffalo, munch on the grass. Enormous elk wander nearby. This was a common sight 200 years ago. But you can still see it today. You're visiting the Elk & Bison Prairie. It's at Land Between the Lakes in southwestern Kentucky.

This area was once rich with wildlife. But hunters wiped out the elk and bison. The herds were built up again in this park.

Kentucky still has lots of wildlife. Forests cover almost half the state. Deer, bobcats, and foxes live there. So do mice, moles, and squirrels. Eagles and hawks soar overhead.

Bison roam the more than 700-acre (238 ha) sanctuary.

HISTORIC CONSTITUTION SQUARE FESTIVAL IN DANVILLE

Make some pottery. Get your face painted. Or take a horse-and-buggy ride. Where is all this going on? At the Historic **Constitution** Square Festival in Danville!

Constitution Square is a famous spot in Kentucky. That's where Kentucky adopted its first constitution. A constitution was required for becoming a state.

But wait—let's back up in time. Great Britain had 13 **colonies** in North America. Present-day Kentucky was part of the Virginia colony. The colonies fought Britain in the Revolutionary War (1775–1783). They won their freedom. Then they became the United States of America. Kentucky separated from Virginia and became a state in 1792.

Kentucky has many festivals to celebrate its heritage. Stop by and see!

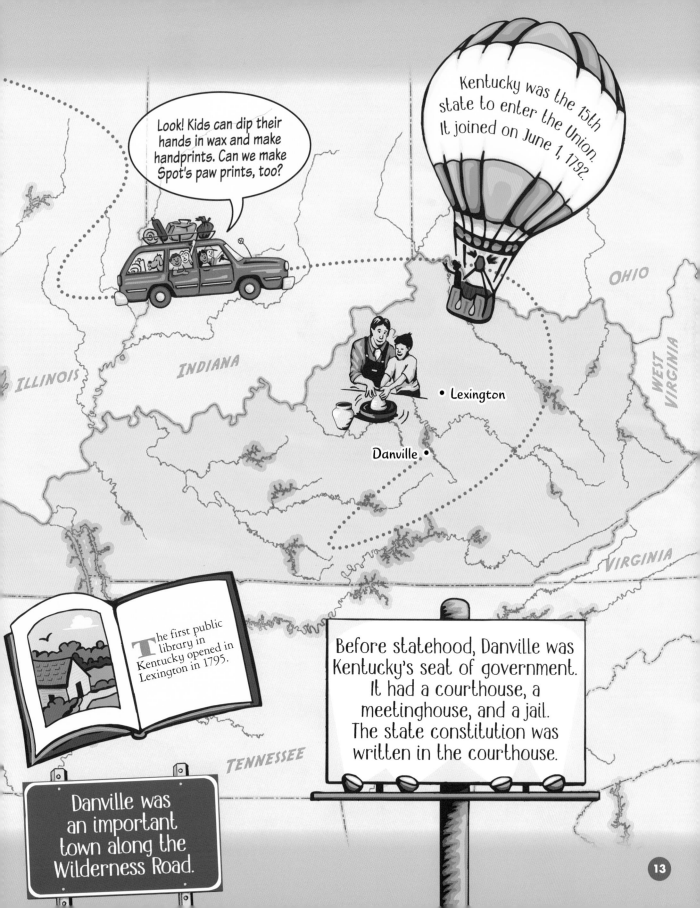

Look! Kids can dip their hands in wax and make handprints. Can we make Spot's paw prints, too?

Kentucky was the 15th state to enter the Union. It joined on June 1, 1792.

OHIO

WEST VIRGINIA

ILLINOIS

INDIANA

• Lexington

Danville •

VIRGINIA

The first public library in Kentucky opened in Lexington in 1795.

Before statehood, Danville was Kentucky's seat of government. It had a courthouse, a meetinghouse, and a jail. The state constitution was written in the courthouse.

TENNESSEE

Danville was an important town along the Wilderness Road.

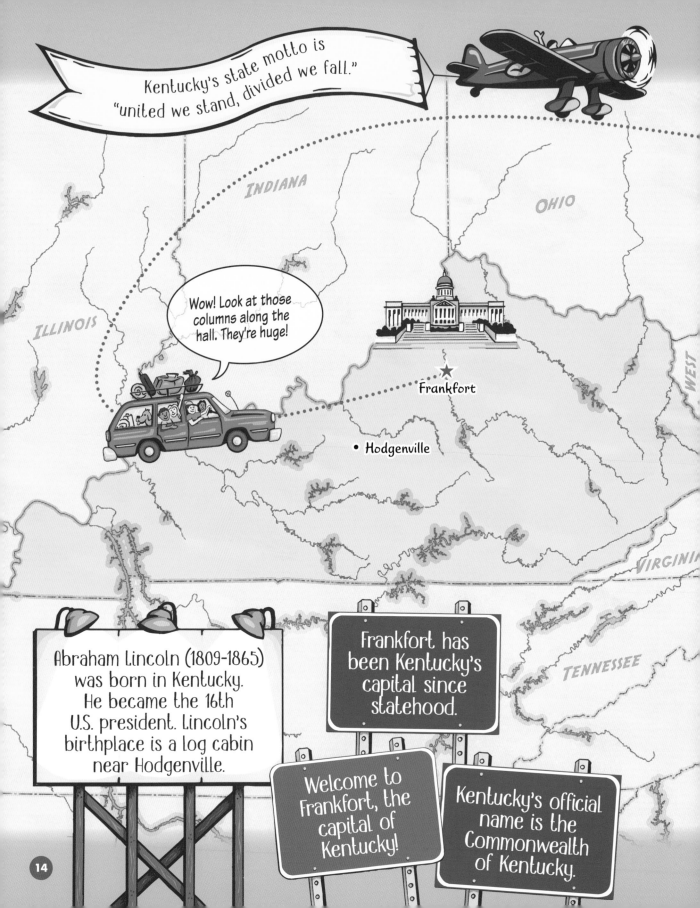

THE STATE CAPITOL IN FRANKFORT

Kentucky's state capitol is very fancy. It's almost like a palace! The center of the building rises up high. There are huge stairways and grand halls. But the builders didn't forget Kentucky's pioneer days. Paintings of Daniel Boone decorate the capitol.

This building houses Kentucky's state government offices. The state government has three branches. One branch is the General Assembly. It makes the state's laws. The governor leads another branch. It carries out the laws. Judges make up the third branch. They decide if someone has broken a law.

Does a king live here? No, this fancy building is the capitol in Frankfort.

SHAKER VILLAGE OF PLEASANT HILL

Walk from one cottage to another. Here's a broom maker. There's a woodworker. Someone else is making butter. You feel like you've stepped back in time!

You're strolling through Shaker Village of Pleasant Hill. Craftspeople are hard at work there. They show how Pleasant Hill villagers once lived.

The Shakers were a religious group. They settled at Pleasant Hill in the early 1800s. They raised crops, fruit trees, and cattle. They made sturdy household goods by hand. High-quality Shaker crafts became famous.

The Shakers changed how brooms were made. This style of broom is from the 1820s.

Look at that farmer. A horse is pulling his plow. There's someone milking a cow. I want to live on a farm!

INDIANA

OHIO

BUTTER

• Washington

• Lexington

• Pleasant Hill

Harrodsburg •

ILLINOIS

WEST VIRGINIA

VIRGINIA

TENNESSEE

Want to know what life was like on a mid-1800s plantation? Visit the Waveland State Historic Site in Lexington.

The village of Washington was founded in 1786. Many of its old log cabins still exist. The town holds a Woodcarver's Day and a Chocolate Festival every year.

Old Fort Harrod is a living-history site in Harrodsburg. It includes costumed guides and craftspeople.

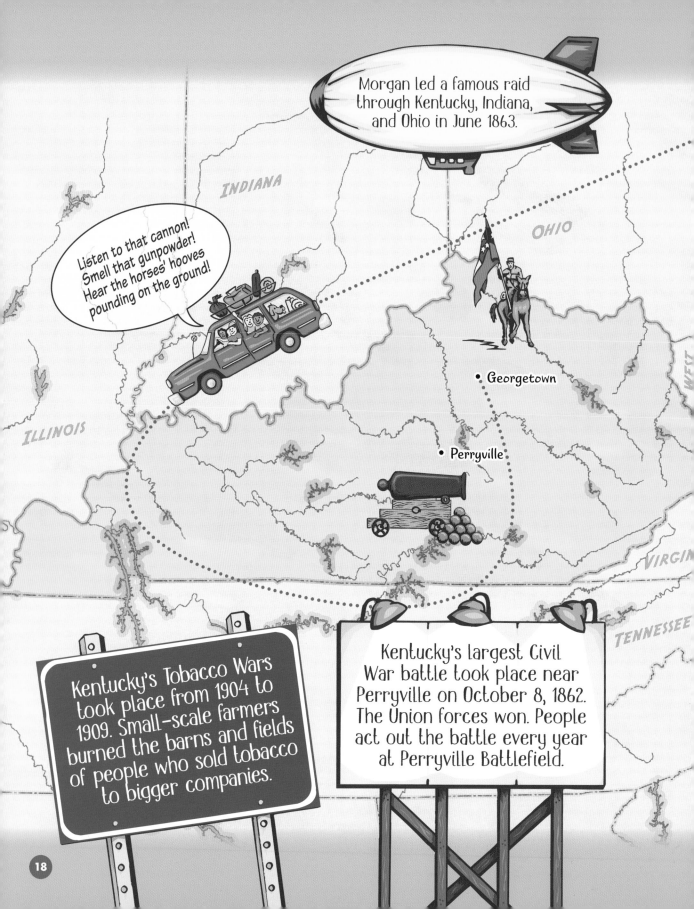

MORGAN'S RAID IN GEORGETOWN

Bang! Pow! Kaboom! Watch out—it's Morgan's Raid!

People in Georgetown act out this battle every year. It took place during the Civil War (1861–1865). The war was between Northern and Southern states. The North, or Union side, was against slavery. Southern states were for it. They formed the Confederacy.

Kentucky didn't want to take sides. It ended up staying in the Union. John Hunt Morgan was a Confederate general. He led several raids in Kentucky. He destroyed Union supplies and caused lots of trouble. Finally, the Union won the war.

John Morgan raided several Kentucky towns. He wanted the South to win the Civil War.

THE WORLD CHICKEN FESTIVAL IN LONDON

First, there's an egg hunt. Then there's an egg-in-a-spoon race. Next? The egg toss and the chicken scratch. You're taking part in the Chick-A-Lympics! It's part of London's World Chicken Festival.

Chickens are an important part of Kentucky's economy. So is tobacco. It's one of Kentucky's leading crops.

Horses are even more important, though. Horse pastures stretch out over the Bluegrass Region. Kentucky horse farms raise thousands of horses. Many horse owners plan to race their animals. Kentucky produces some of the world's fastest racehorses!

Cluck, cluck, cluck! Couldn't have the Chicken Festival without Kentucky's chickens!

In 2016, 4,436,974 people lived in Kentucky. It's the 26th-largest state by population.

I want to see the metal kitty and the walking sticks!

INDIANA

OHIO

ILLINOIS

• Louisville

• Morehead

• Lexington

Appalachian Region

WEST

• Bowling Green

VIRGINIA

Kentucky musician Bill Monroe started the Blue Grass Boys band in the 1930s. Their style of music came to be called bluegrass music.

POPULATION OF LARGEST CITIES
Lexington.....................314,488
Louisville.....................615,366
Bowling Green..............63,616

TENNESSEE

Louisville holds the Corn Island Storytelling Festival and the Bluegrass and Bourbon Experience in September.

THE KENTUCKY FOLK ART CENTER IN MOREHEAD

You catch a glimpse of long-necked blue roosters. You even see the famous Wild Booger! Don't worry—they're just pieces of art. You're touring the Kentucky **Folk Art** Center in Morehead. It features unusual art from the Appalachian Region.

Kentuckians enjoy many local arts and crafts. Many people make quilts and pottery. They follow patterns handed down over many years. Bluegrass music had its start in Kentucky. Country music and folk songs are popular, too.

Most residents used to live in the country. Now most Kentuckians live in cities or towns. But they still honor their country roots.

Bluegrass music is a type of art that's celebrated in Kentucky.

THE MINI CORVETTE CHALLENGE IN BOWLING GREEN

Are you crazy about Corvettes? These sporty little cars are really sharp! Just check out the Junior Achievement Mini Corvette Challenge. It's a go-cart race. But the go-carts have Corvette bodies! The race is in Bowling Green. That's where Corvettes are made.

Kentucky relied on farming for a long time. Tobacco and horses brought in lots of income. Miners dug tons of coal from Kentucky's mines, too.

Farming and mining slowed down by the 1950s. Manufacturing was growing fast, though. Many car factories opened in Kentucky. Now cars are made in Georgetown and Louisville. And don't forget Bowling Green and its Corvettes!

Are you a fan of sports cars? Then check out the National Corvette Museum in Bowling Green!

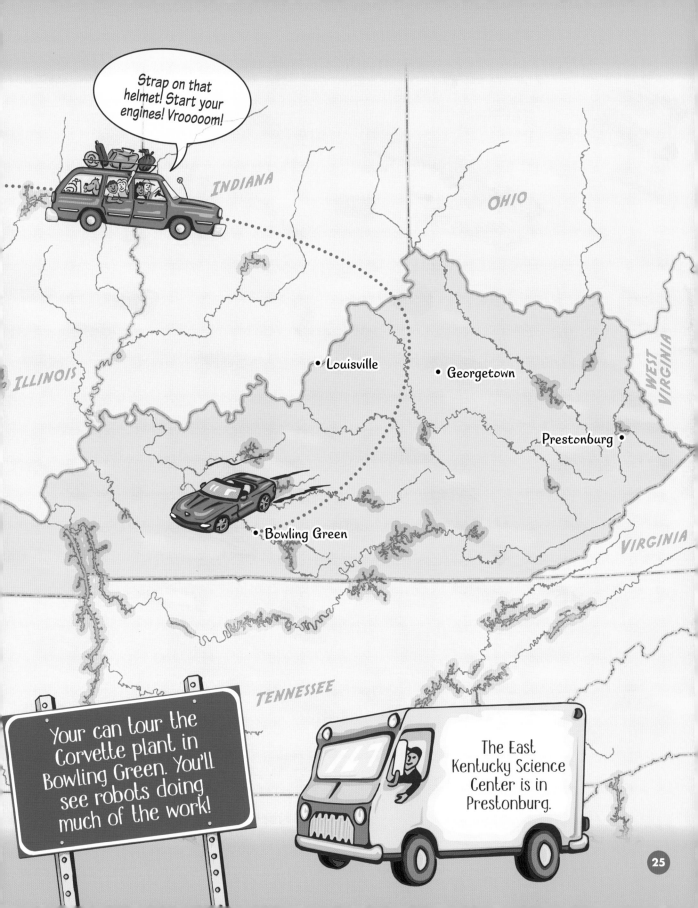

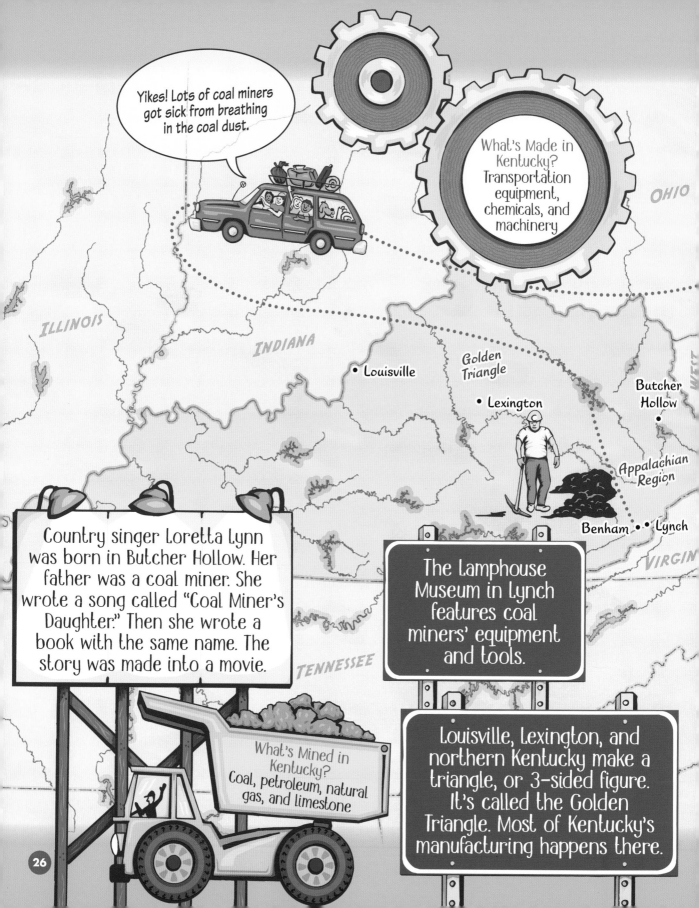

The winding path is dark and spooky. You feel like you're deep underground. You're touring a model of a coal mine. It's in Benham's Kentucky Coal Mining Museum.

Kentucky is a top coal mining state. It has two main coal-mining regions. One is in the far northwest. The other is in the eastern Appalachian Region.

Kentucky has lots of big factories, too. Cars and trucks are the major factory products. Many factories make car and truck parts. Other factories make medicine, paint, and machinery.

Coal is mostly used for electricity. Learn all about how it is mined.

THE KENTUCKY DERBY AT CHURCHILL DOWNS

And they're off! The horses dash out of the gate. 'Round the track they go. Your favorite is pulling ahead!

You're at the country's most exciting horse race. It's the Kentucky Derby at Churchill Downs. This race is Kentucky's biggest sports event. It happens on the first Saturday in May. People come from around the world to watch.

Many Kentuckians also enjoy baseball. They cross the northern border into Ohio. There they can watch Cincinnati Reds games.

Kentuckians also love the great outdoors. Some go fishing, boating, or camping. Others explore caves or hike through the mountains. As you see, there's plenty to do in Kentucky!

Twenty horses run in the Kentucky Derby every year.

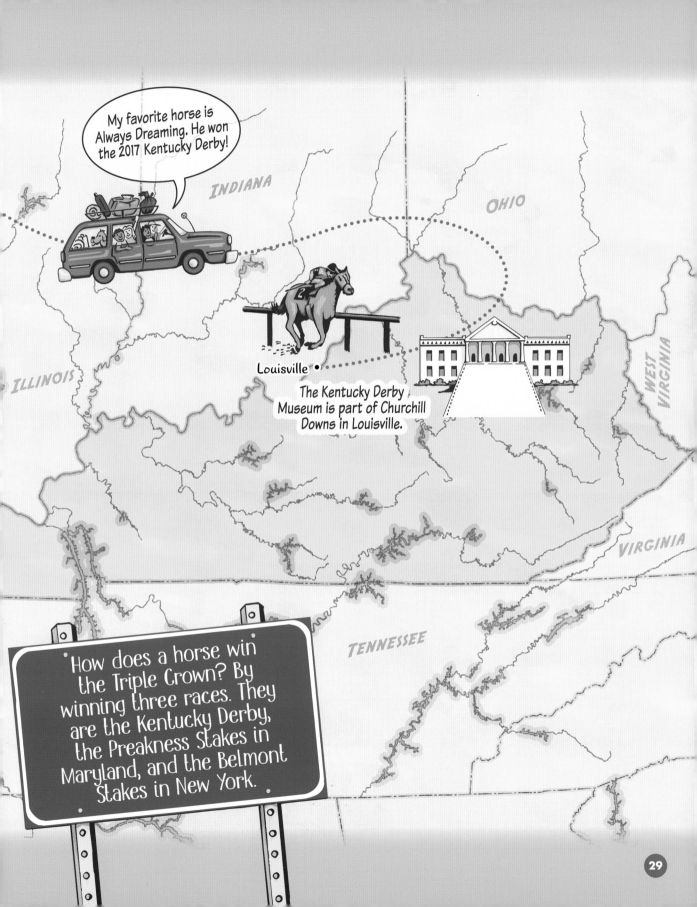

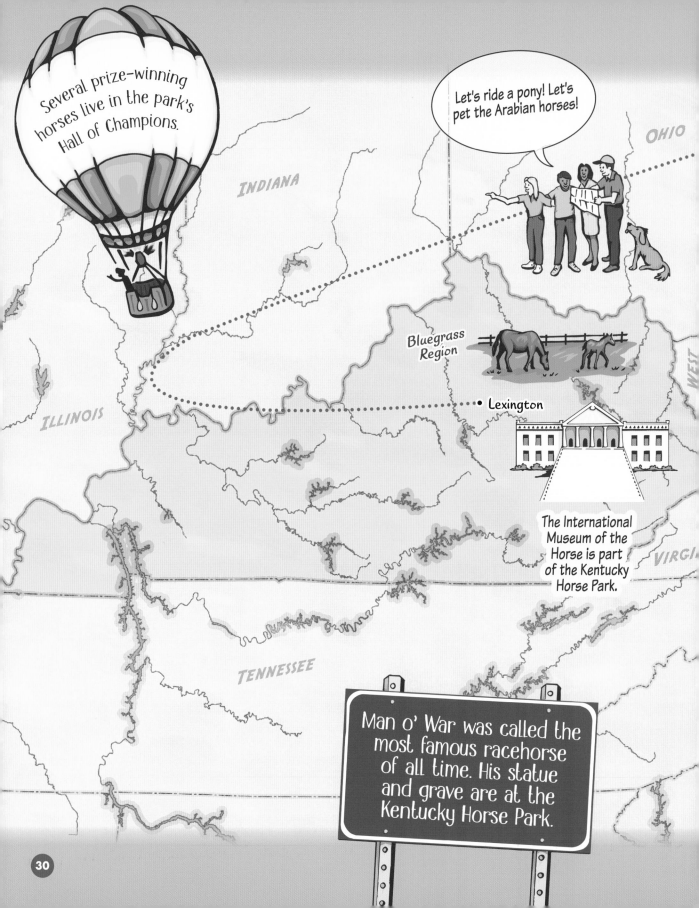

KENTUCKY HORSE PARK IN LEXINGTON

SECRETARIAT

White fences surround acres of pasture. Beautiful horses trot around or just graze. This is Lexington's Kentucky Horse Park. It's in the heart of Kentucky's Bluegrass Region.

You'll see almost 50 breeds of horses at the park. They hold horse shows in the summer. Many breeds perform there.

One barn is a home for draft horses. These are horses that pull heavy loads. You can tour the park in a horse-drawn carriage. It's pulled by draft horses. A blacksmith works at the park, too. He pounds out iron to make horseshoes.

Kentucky Horse Park has many museums and exhibits. If you love horses, it's the place for you!

Secretariat is another famous racehorse. There is a statue of him at Lexington's Kentucky Horse Park.

THE U.S. BULLION DEPOSITORY AT FORT KNOX

Bars of gold are stacked to the ceiling. They're worth billions of dollars! Just one bar is worth more than $16,000!

This is the U.S. gold **depository**. It's a well-guarded building in Fort Knox. The U.S. government stores much of its gold there. You'll never get near that gold, though. No visitors are allowed. Still, it's fun to think about!

This building is very strong and safe. It was useful during World War II (1939–1945). Many important items were stored there. One was the U.S. Declaration of Independence. Others included Great Britain's crown jewels. These jewels belong to the royal family.

Fort Knox is home to billions of dollars in gold.

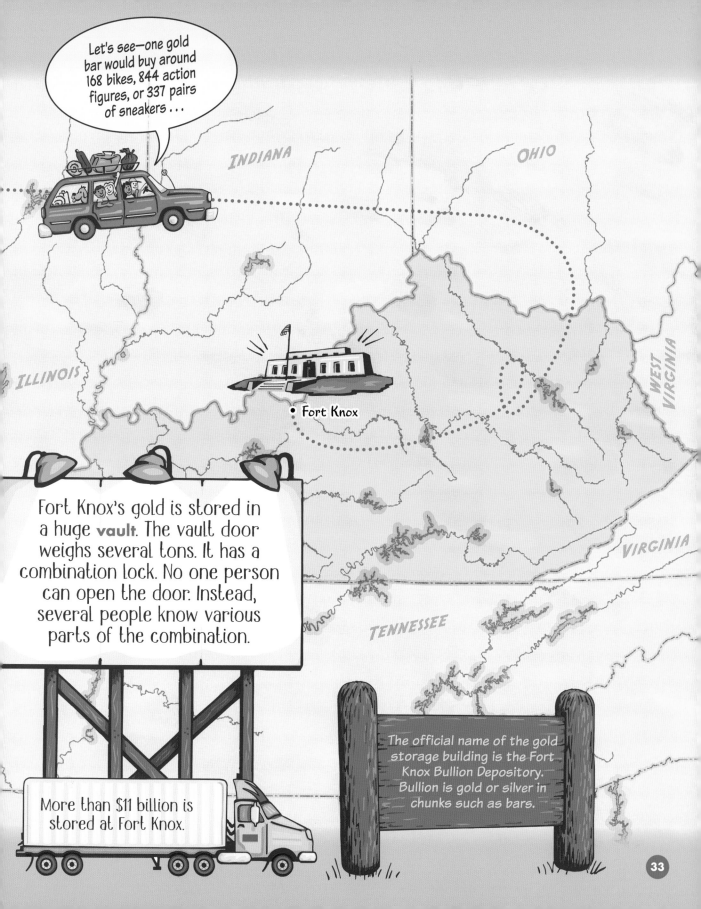

Let's see—one gold bar would buy around 168 bikes, 844 action figures, or 337 pairs of sneakers . . .

INDIANA

OHIO

ILLINOIS

WEST VIRGINIA

• Fort Knox

Fort Knox's gold is stored in a huge **vault**. The vault door weighs several tons. It has a combination lock. No one person can open the door. Instead, several people know various parts of the combination.

VIRGINIA

TENNESSEE

The official name of the gold storage building is the Fort Knox Bullion Depository. Bullion is gold or silver in chunks such as bars.

More than $11 billion is stored at Fort Knox.

THE GREAT OUTHOUSE BLOWOUT IN GRAVEL SWITCH

The announcer yells to begin the race. "Ladies and gentlemen, start your toilets!" You're in the tiny town of Gravel Switch. And you're watching the Great Outhouse Blowout. It's an outhouse race!

An outhouse is an outdoor restroom. It's shaped like a phone booth. Outhouses were used before people had indoor plumbing.

The race has lots of rules. Each outhouse has to have a name. All outhouses must roll on wheels. A five-person team races each outhouse. Two people push it. Two people pull it. And one person rides inside.

Winning the race isn't everything. There's also an award for the most creative outhouse!

Travel to Gravel Switch to see the outhouse races!

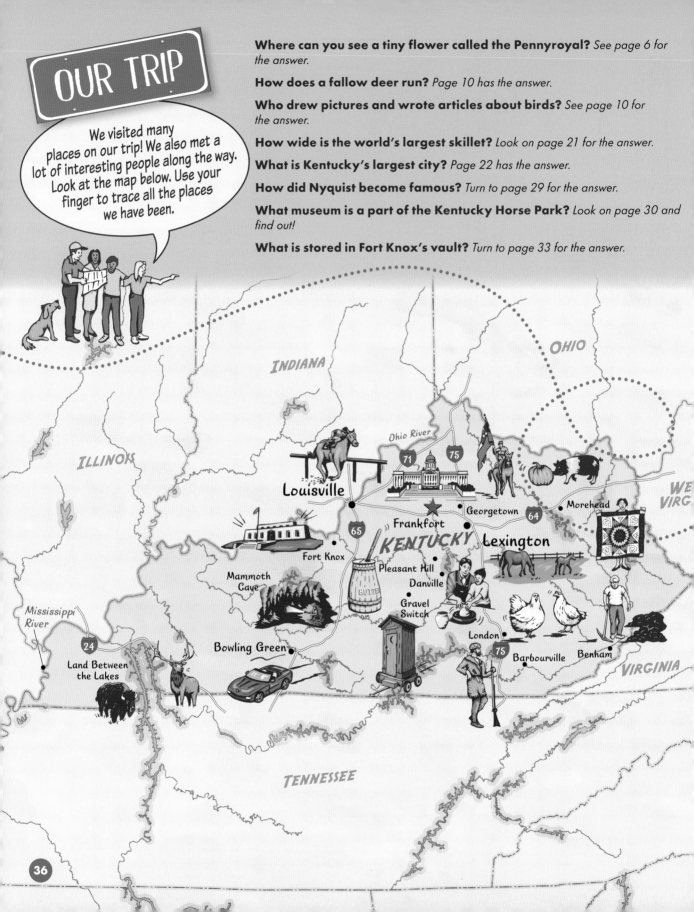

OUR TRIP

We visited many places on our trip! We also met a lot of interesting people along the way. Look at the map below. Use your finger to trace all the places we have been.

Where can you see a tiny flower called the Pennyroyal? *See page 6 for the answer.*

How does a fallow deer run? *Page 10 has the answer.*

Who drew pictures and wrote articles about birds? *See page 10 for the answer.*

How wide is the world's largest skillet? *Look on page 21 for the answer.*

What is Kentucky's largest city? *Page 22 has the answer.*

How did Nyquist become famous? *Turn to page 29 for the answer.*

What museum is a part of the Kentucky Horse Park? *Look on page 30 and find out!*

What is stored in Fort Knox's vault? *Turn to page 33 for the answer.*

INDIANA

OHIO

ILLINOIS

Ohio River

WE VIRG.

Louisville

Frankfort

Georgetown

Morehead

KENTUCKY

Lexington

Fort Knox

Pleasant Hill

Mammoth Cave

Danville

Mississippi River

Gravel Switch

London

Land Between the Lakes

Bowling Green

Barbourville

Benham

VIRGINIA

TENNESSEE

State flag

State seal

That was a great trip! We have traveled all over Kentucky! There are a few places that we didn't have time for, though. Next time, we plan to visit the Double Stink Hog Farm in Georgetown. This famous farm used to raise pigs and other animals. But now visitors come to enjoy the sweet corn and pumpkins!

STATE SYMBOLS

State bird: Northern Cardinal

State bluegrass song: "Blue Moon of Kentucky"

State butterfly: Viceroy butterfly

State fish: Kentucky spotted bass

State flower: Goldenrod

State fossil: Brachiopod

State gemstone: Freshwater pearl

State horse: Thoroughbred

State tree: Tulip poplar

State wild game animal: Gray squirrel

STATE SONG

"MY OLD KENTUCKY HOME"
Words and music by Stephen Collins Foster

The Sun shines bright in my old Kentucky
  home,
'Tis summer, the people are gay;
The corn top's ripe and the meadow's in
  the bloom,
While the birds make music all the day.

The young folks roll on the little cabin
  floor,
All merry, all happy and bright;
By 'n by hard times comes a-knocking at
  the door,
Then my old Kentucky home, good night!

Chorus:
Weep no more, my lady
Oh weep no more today;
We will sing one song
For my old Kentucky home,
For my old Kentucky home, far away.

FAMOUS PEOPLE

Ali, Muhammad (1942–2016), boxer

Boone, Daniel (1734–1820), pioneer

Breckinridge, John Cabell (1821–1875), U.S. vice president

Breckinridge, Madeline McDowell (1872–1920), women's rights activist

Clay, Henry (1777–1852), politician

Clooney, George (1961–), actor

Depp, Johnny (1963–), actor

Griffith, D. W. (1875–1948), film director

Handy, W. C. (1873–1958), blues musician

Judd, Ashley (1968–), actor

King, Pee Wee (1914–2000), country music performer

Lawrence, Jennifer (1990–), actress

Lincoln, Abraham (1809–1865), 16th U.S. president

Lynn, Loretta (1932–), singer

Mason, Bobbie Ann (1940–), author

Monroe, Rose Will ("Rosie the Riveter") (1920–1997), American feminist hero

Powers, Georgia (1923–), Kentucky's first female state senator and first African-American state senator

Sharp, Philip A. (1944–), biologist and Nobel Peace Price winner

Stevenson, Adlai E. (1835–1914), U.S. vice president

Thompson, Hunter S. (1939–2005), author

Young, Whitney M., Jr. (1921–1971), civil rights leader

WORDS TO KNOW

breeches (BRICH-iz) knee-length pants that are tight at the bottom

colonies (KOL-uh-neez) new lands with ties to a parent country

constitution (kon-stuh-TOO-shuhn) a basic set of laws for a country or state

depository (di-POZ-i-tor-ee) a place where things are stored

folk art (FOHK ART) art by people who have little or no artistic training

frontiersman (fruhn-TIHRZ-man) someone who is skilled at living and traveling in an unexplored, forested region

hard hat (HARD HAT) a hat made of hard material to protect the head

pioneer (pye-uh-NEER) someone who moves into an unsettled area

plantation (plan-TAY-shuhn) a large farm that raises crops

vault (VAWLT) a room where money and other valuables are stored

TO LEARN MORE

IN THE LIBRARY

Edgar, Sherra. *What's Great About Kentucky?* Minneapolis, MN: Lerner Publications, 2015.

Glaser, Jason. *Kentucky: The Bluegrass State.* New York, NY: PowerKids Press, 2010.

Wilbur, Helen. *D is for Derby: A Kentucky Derby Alphabet.* Ann Arbor, MI: Sleeping Bear Press, 2014.

ON THE WEB

Visit our Web site for links about Kentucky:

childsworld.com/links

Note to Parents, Teachers, and Librarians: We routinely verify our Web links to make sure they are safe and active sites. So encourage your readers to check them out!

PLACES TO VISIT OR CONTACT

The Kentucky Department of Travel

kentuckytourism.com
100 Airport Road, 2nd floor
Frankfort, KY 40601
800/225-8747
For more information about traveling in Kentucky

Kentucky Historical Society

history.ky.gov
100 W. Broadway
Frankfort, KY 40601
502/564-1792
For more information about the history of Kentucky

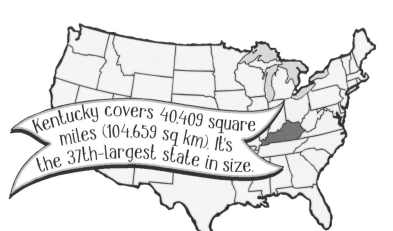

Kentucky covers 40,409 square miles (104,659 sq km). It's the 37th-largest state in size.

INDEX

Bye, Bluegrass State.
We had a great time.
We'll come back soon!